A Tale of Two Towns

To the traveller heading south over the great downland Ridgeway from Dorchester a magnificent panorama unfolds. Spread out below, with the sea on either side and only the intriguing profile of the Island of Portland to break the horizon, lies what was formerly the 'Borough of Weymouth and Melcombe Regis'.

The setting is glorious, for there is much more to Weymouth than its famous beach and reputation as one of the sunniest places in Britain. The old buildings, the Harbour busy with boats, the great variety of the surrounding villages, all combine to make the area round Weymouth fascinating to explore.

Either side of the town is the newly designated

Osmington Hill provides a fine first view of Weymouth, with its sheltered bay bordered by the gentle sweep of the beach.

UNESCO Dorset and East Devon Coast World Heritage Site, popularly called 'The Jurassic Coast'. The shoreline from east Devon to the Purbecks provides a near continuous geological record of the entire 'Middle Period' of the earth's ancient history, spanning the period between 251 and 66 million years ago – a presentation of past environments not equalled anywhere else in the world.

The heights of the Ridgeway dominate the lower-lying coastal plain occupied by Weymouth. They extend from White Horse Hill in the east to Abbotsbury Hill in the west. An ancient trackway (the 'Ridge Way') crosses the top of this chalky hill-range, passing numerous prehistoric earthworks, whilst the old Roman road from Durnovaria (Dorchester) can still be traced descending the Weymouth side of the escarpment.

Many springs emerge along the foot of the Ridgeway, which widen into streams and meander southward to the sea. Their water is copious and clear. Five of them drain into the Fleet, the long brackish lagoon that divides the Chesil Beach from the mainland. The 'river' Jordon runs from Sutton Poyntz down to Bowleaze Cove, Preston Brook rises in the delightful Coombe Valley and discharges to Lodmoor, while the four mile long River Wey and its tributaries reach the sea via Radipole Lake and the Harbour.

The town of Weymouth originated along the northern side of the ridge fronting the Harbour, between Boot Hill and Hope Square, probably well before the arrival of the Normans in 1066. Facing it on the other side of the Harbour, the separate town of Melcombe originated as a small group of houses near

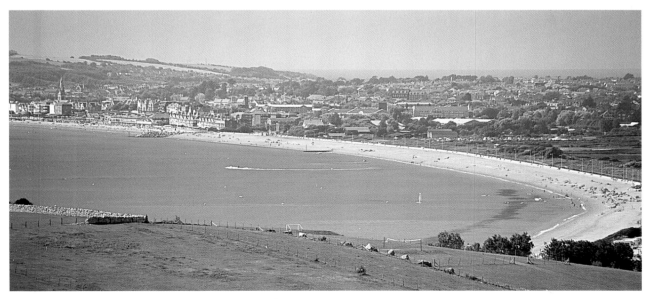

the water's edge, only accessible by tracks over the sandbanks from the north. Thus, and confusingly, what we now think of as Weymouth began life as Melcombe, whilst Melcombe itself only survives as a name.

Old Weymouth's buildings and narrow streets were constrained by the lack of space between the escarpment and the water. In contrast, the medieval builders of Melcombe Regis had low flat land on which to establish the grid-pattern of streets which is still seen today. ('Regis' was added to its name in the fourteenth century, and the land remained owned by the Crown until given to the borough by Queen Elizabeth I). Generations of quay walls and wharves were built, and a rope-ferry plied across the water.

For centuries the two towns were in conflict over use of the Harbour, but in 1347 they managed to patch up their differences long enough to provide 20 ships for the siege of Calais, at the start of the Hundred Years War. The following summer brought catastrophe. A mariner from Europe afflicted with plague landed at Melcombe. This was no ordinary plague. The Black Death spread rapidly and spared no one, and by the time the final graves had been dug it had claimed the lives of a third of the population: perhaps three million. This was followed by numerous French raids on the port, which virtually wiped out trade, and reduced the area to poverty.

It took two centuries and the setting aside of petty rivalries for the two towns to regain their prosperity. In 1571 they were formed into a single borough. Shortly afterwards, as if to symbolize their union, a wooden bridge was built over the Harbour, linking the two communities. The present Town Bridge, of Portland Stone, has a lifting deck whose two arms are raised several times a day to allow larger vessels to move to and from the Marina. It was opened by the Duke of York (later King George VI) in 1930, replacing a narrow stone-and-iron swing structure which had served the town since 1824.

Today's Harbour waterfront, with its shops,

A rolling pastoral landscape viewed from Plaisters Lane. Earthworks of an ancient hill fort on Chalbury Hill, right, command a spectacular view towards the Island of Portland on the distant horizon.

The Old Town Hall, near the equally historic Boot Inn, dates from Tudor times, when Weymouth was just a small town on the south side of the harbour.

restaurants and pubs, is full of character. Facing the bridge is the soaring front of Holy Trinity Church, complete with underground catacombs, which was built in 1836 and positioned so as to give as much impact as possible. Architecturally the Harbour reflects the various phases when it was at its busiest and most prosperous. There have been some sad losses: in the 1960s the entire old Weymouth High Street, including some Tudor housing, was cleared to make way for the featureless Council Offices block. In contrast along Trinity Road and the streets around the eastern end, are carefully restored terraces of intermixed Victorian, Georgian and earlier buildings, their backs tightly pressed against the cliff face. Trinity Street has a rare gem, the restored Tudor House, which visitors can see inside just as it was when it was the home of a 16th century merchant.

Sheltered Waters

Weymouth Marina – the Inner Harbour below Westham Bridge – has been dramatically transformed since it was the town's 'Backwater'. From 1834 when a huge gasworks was built, the mud banks on both sides have been reclaimed by the building of quay walls and harbourside roads. In the last years of the twentieth century the waterfront has changed beyond recognition. Where once it was dominated by timber ponds, warehouses, ship yards, and the profusion of workshops and businesses associated with a bustling port, now smart apartments and a shopping centre look out over one of the most sheltered marinas on the south coast.

Foreign shipping regularly moored alongside Weymouth's waterfront from the early eighteenth century. It was also the home port of a handful of

The Harbour is still used commercially, and fishing remains a vital industry, but leisure now predominates. Beyond the small boats is a replica of the eighteenth century explorer James Cook's barque *Endeavour*. The scene is truly spectacular when the tall ships visit this area.

Nothe Parade is one of the most picturesque frontages of Weymouth Harbour. The narrow quayside road leads past the lifeboat station to Nothe Gardens and the Stone Pier.

ships trading with Newfoundland, and several of the large warehouses on the harbourside date from this period. Many of these historic buildings have now very different uses: An example is the Deep Sea Adventure on Custom House Quay, where underwater exploration from the 17th century is depicted, together with an acclaimed Titanic exhibition. Weymouth has the shortest sea route to the Channel Islands, and there have been regular maritime services between the two since the Middle Ages. The introduction of the post office packet service to the Islands in 1794 started a new era in the port's prosperity. The link was never without problems: many sailing vessels were lost in the stormy Channel, and early packets were even armed to counter attacks from the French during the Napoleonic wars. In due course the packets were replaced by three steamer paddle boats. But their engines were notoriously unreliable, and their captains often had hoisted their trusty schooner-rigged sails – the old salts had more faith in canvas than coal!

Despite Weymouth's small tidal range, major work was needed to build up and retain strong working quays, to accommodate the ever-increasing size of vessels using the port. The arrival of the railway in

1857 was soon followed by branch lines to both Portland and along the Harbour's edge to the commercial pier. The 'Weymouth Quay Tramway' gave passengers and goods direct access to ferries and cargo vessels. Trade with the Channel Islands expanded, and the enlargement of piers and shore facilities continued through the twentieth century. The Great Western Railway took on the Channel Islands run in 1889, which went from strength to strength. Fruit, vegetables and flowers were the major imports, and when in season 100 tons of daffodils and 50,000 packages of tomatoes a day were being landed

in open boxes on the quayside at Weymouth. The presence of a railway capable of carrying mainline trains along rails in a busy street to the quay never ceased to amaze visitors. There is no longer any regular service on this line, but the occasional 'special' train draws countrywide interest.

The Second World War brought drama and movement on an unprecedented scale as the ports of Weymouth and Portland became embarkation points for hundreds of thousands of allied troops and their vehicles, bound for the great D-Day assault on Normandy. A plaque on Weymouth's seafront War Memorial commemorates the local people lost in the historic conflict, while an eternal lamp atop a column opposite the Royal Hotel was erected in 1947 as a tribute to the fallen Americans. After the war Weymouth became a lifeline for commercial trade

Heading seaward for a night sail. The twin leaves of the Town Bridge are raised several times a day for navigation to and from the Weymouth Marina.

from the liberated Channel Islands, importing more than 1 million tons in 1946.

Containerisation at larger rival ports eventually put an end to the frantic quayside bustle. The huge steel cranes have gone, and there could be no greater contrast than that between the sedate steamers of old and the sleek hydrofoil ferries introduced in 1987. But the days of sail are certainly not over. Alongside the commercial fishing boats, Weymouth is a magnet for hundreds of leisure craft from all over the Europe, and when the magnificent 'tall ships' of the world put into port, the scene in the Bay and Harbour is spectacular.

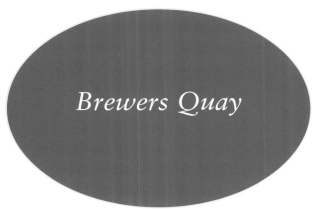

Brewers Quay

Hope Square, by Brewers Quay, was originally an inlet - an 'ope' - of the Harbour, which was infilled towards the end of the eighteenth century. By 1817 several rows of houses had been built over it, some of which were demolished in the 1880s when the Harbour was widened to enable large steamers to swing around. Dominating this part of the town is a group of cavernous Victorian breweries and malthouses, whose brick chimney stack towers over the surrounding roofs.

For centuries the area was characterised by an industrial atmosphere of the most pleasant kind: the clang of barrels and rhythmic thump of coopers' hammers, the clatter of hooves, the shouts of men loading drays, and the all pervading strong, sweet aroma of malt in the air.

Transformation came in the last decade of the twentieth century after brewing had stopped, and this former working area became filled with cafés, pubs, charming little shops and art galleries. Visitors now throng to the colourful block-paved square and waterside streets for refreshment and entertainment. The huge malthouses have been cleverly converted to apartments and the brewery itself has been imaginatively redeveloped into the award winning 'Timewalk', where by the use of the latest technology visitors are taken on a vivid journey through 600 years of Weymouth and Portland's history. In another part, old machinery and artefacts with animated displays bring the old brewery to life. Here also is the Weymouth Museum, a fascinating treasure-house of objects and archive documents relating to the town's past.

LEFT The formidable Victorian brewery buildings at Hope Square have been transformed into the Brewers Quay leisure complex. Inside are the Weymouth Timewalk historical experience, Weymouth Museum, restaurants and shops.

BELOW Craft workshops in the shadow of the old brewery chimney. This is all part of the extensive Brewers Quay attraction near the Hope Square harbourside.

The Nothe

Nothe Parade is one of the quaintest parts of the Harbour. Striking out from the Nothe peninsula is the Stone Pier, a rebuilding of an ancient structure giving vital shelter to the Harbour entrance against prevailing seas. Weymouth Lifeboat Station and the range of historic houses fronting the Parade's narrow roadway add to its attractions. It used to be a working quay - among the boats launched by Ayles' shipbuilding yard here was the 125 ton schooner *Portland*, in 1827.

Weymouth's latest lifeboat, the *Ernest and Mabel*, took up station in September 2002. She is the latest and most powerful in a proud line of vessels dating back to 1869 when the port's first lifeboat was commissioned. Until the first motor lifeboat arrived in 1924 all the craft were powered by oars and sail. It was – and still is – a fearsome task for the volunteer crews to attend stricken vessels in the notoriously rough Race off Portland, well beyond the relatively sheltered waters of Weymouth Bay.

Weymouth and its neighbour Portland, due to their

ABOVE Construction of the Nothe Fort began in 1860. It was continually developed to make use of rapidly evolving ordnance technology, right up to the S econd World War. Now visitors can explore its ramparts, casemates and underground passages.

BELOW Anglers and strollers enjoy the late evening sun on the Stone Pier.

location, have always been vulnerable to attack from across the Channel. The area also experienced fighting during the Civil War in the seventeenth century, and witnessed action between the English fleet and Spanish Armada just off this coast.

Victorian Royal Engineers built the Nothe Fort to command the approaches to Weymouth Harbour.

Lifesavers to the rescue! Weymouth Lifeboat the *Ernest and Mabel*, commissioned in 2002, and Portland Coastguard Helicopter - the country's busiest - are put through their paces off the Nothe.

The steep-sided rock promontory of the Nothe gives excellent natural protection to the Harbour mouth. It was a superb vantage point for the defence of the town and its approaches, so gun batteries were mounted here from the earliest days of ordnance.

1849 saw the start of one of Victorian Britain's greatest engineering projects. The anchorage of 'Portland Roads', south of Weymouth, was developed into a vast harbour of refuge for the nation's burgeoning navy and merchant ships. Portland Harbour was formed by the construction of enormous stone breakwaters. The scheme took half a century to complete and had a great and lasting impact on the development of Portland and Weymouth. Following the thousands of engineers, administrators – and convicts to quarry the stone, came tourists by the trainload.

To defend this new harbour and its approaches from a prospective enemy – the French remained a fearful threat – a range of coastal defences was planned. Three great fortresses were built; on the Nothe, on Portland's Verne Hill, and on the new Breakwater itself. Designed by the Royal Engineers, they were all incredible feats of ingenuity and engineering skill. For twelve years from 1860 the rocky headland was the scene of frenetic activity while the Nothe Fort was developed. Protected by massive sea- and retaining walls, its formidable defences contain more than 70 rooms on three levels. Heavy guns were mounted above and within its ramparts to sweep the coast, cross-firing with those on the Portland forts. As with so many of its contemporaries, the detailing of its massive Portland Stone masonry has a striking beauty.

Nothe Fort saw much activity during the Second World War when Weymouth and Portland were under frequent air attack. It remained in military hands until 1961, when it was sold to the Weymouth Council. Plans were drawn up to convert it into a luxury hotel, and construction work actually started. That work was abruptly abandoned and dereliction set in until the Council started restoration work in 1978. A year later the enterprise was taken over by Weymouth Civic Society, whose 25 years of enthusiastic voluntary effort has safeguarded a remarkable historical feature. Nothe Fort is now one of Dorset's premier attractions, with more than 60,000 visitors a year experiencing the sights, sounds - and smells - of its bygone military atmosphere. Moving models of ships and aircraft, dioramas, displays of naval battles, real and replica artillery make this an entertaining and educational experience for both young and old.

The whole headland, once under military occupation, is now dedicated to peaceful enjoyment, and recreation. The beautifully landscaped Nothe Gardens extend right over the peninsula from Harbour to southern shore, where in 2003 a new promenade to Newtons Cove has added yet another major amenity to the town.

Georgian Splendour

From every vantage, the eye is drawn along the gentle sweep of Weymouth Bay. The sands at the southern end merge into a fine shingle towards Greenhill, and northward along the recently enlarged beach to Overcombe. This south-east facing beach is ideally situated to catch the morning sun, warming the shallow waters ready for paddlers and bathers.

From a distance the long, grand Georgian terraces have a delightful symmetry. They form a perfect backdrop, and their continuity makes an effective break to the prevailing westerly breezes. Most bathing beaches look seaward to a featureless horizon, but not here. Instead there is the distant roller-coaster of the green-topped white cliffs of the south Dorset coast; undoubtedly one of the most pleasant coastal scenes in the country.

The vista has long inspired artists. The celebrated J.M.W. Turner produced a delightful watercolour of the beach on his visit in 1811, at a time when several of the great Georgian terraces were still under construction. Five years later John Constable, on honeymoon at nearby Osmington with his wife Maria, produced a series of fine paintings of Weymouth Bay and the coves.

Had either of the two artists arrived even thirty years earlier, their brushes would have recorded a very different view. The town consisted of little more than a cluster of buildings near the Harbour, around the lower parts of St Nicholas, St Edmund, St Thomas and St Mary Streets - names first recorded in 1318. The seaward side was considered of little value; parts of the beach were used as a rubbish dump.

OPPOSITE PAGE Floral decorations on the Georgian bow-windows of Brunswick Terrace enhance the sunny seafront setting.

BELOW The evening lights of Weymouth seafront, glimpsed between the trees in Nothe Gardens which overlook the Harbour.

To the north there were a few buildings on the low shingle isthmus called The Narrows between the Bay and the Backwater. The beach there was exposed to winds blowing over the Backwater, and the scattering of low-lying houses facing the sea – in what is now Crescent Street – had no wall to protect them from waves breaking over the summit of the beach.

All that changed after the carriage carrying King George III from London first descended the rough road down the hillside towards Weymouth. His brother, the Duke of Gloucester, had already discovered the delights of this beautiful and unspoilt watering place, when in 1780 he chose a prime position facing the beach to build Gloucester Lodge. Encouraged to try sea-bathing for his own health, the king came to stay there nine years later. He enjoyed the experience so much that he spent 14 extended holidays in the town between 1789 and 1805.

Along with his Queen, Charlotte, and his many children, there came a whole army of servants, courtiers, gentry and affluent visitors, for whom accommodation had to be provided. Entrepreneurs rose to the occasion, and local architects led by the prolific James Hamilton produced the grand vision for a new sea front development for the town. By the turn of the nineteenth century the land behind Weymouth's beach was a scene of building frenzy as enormous quantities of Portland stone, bricks, timber and slates arrived by barge and haulage cart. Over the next few decades hundreds of skilled craftsmen, and labourers busy with barrows, wooden scaffolding and hoists, built one of England's finest classic esplanades.

The designs had to satisfy more than aesthetics. To erect great continuous terraces on loose gravely land was a formidable structural challenge. Most of the large buildings have basements excavated almost to sea level, and rise to 3 or 4 storeys above ground. The four most prominent terraces have perfectly rounded ends - an architectural inspiration which softens the vista. It is testimony to some far-sighted Georgian, Regency and Victorian minds that we can still appreciate their majestic work after nearly two centuries.

The Esplanade we now see was largely completed by 1855. Originally lined with private houses for the fashionable, most were converted into hotels and guest houses for a new generation of tourists who arrived en masse after the arrival of the railway. The terminus disgorged the visitors just a short walk from the beach.

Esplanade of elegance. Although Belvedere Terrace was started during the Regency (1818) and completed in the Victorian age (1855), its designer maintained the Georgian theme set by Royal Crescent of 1805, off to the left.

The separate Sea Front terraces merge into a continuous
backdrop when seen from the beach at low tide.

For nearly 200 years this imposing statue of George III
has taken pride of place in his favourite resort.

The long summers of the Royal visits were fully
described in the newspapers of the time. People came
from all over the country to imitate their monarch –
to enjoy promenading, concerts, theatre, rides in the
countryside and to Portland – but the raison d'être
was always sea bathing.

Weymouth was launched on its greatest and most
prosperous period. For a while it was the most
fashionable town in the country. In honour of their
royal patron, its citizens commissioned a large statue
of George III, resplendent in his robes, to stand on an
enormous plinth of Portland stone. The stoneware
figure, modelled from life, was cast in London and
brought to the town by ship in 1804. It was then
stored for 5 years before a location for it was agreed,
facing along his beloved sea front. Princess Mary laid
the foundation stone in October 1809, when corn, oil
and wine were sprinkled on the mortar, and the
celebrations and fireworks went on into the night. A
year later the completed King's Statue, guarded by a
magnificent golden lion and white unicorn, was
unveiled. The name of 'J. Hamilton Archt.', whose
architecture embodies Georgian Weymouth, is rightly
included in the bold inscription on the plinth.

As well as designing three of Weymouth's seafront
terraces, and producing the sketch for the chalk figure

of the king on horseback cut in the side of Osmington Hill, Hamilton went on to design St. Mary's Church, completed in 1817. It is in the same part of St Mary Street where once stood an ancient friary, then in 1605 the first church. St Mary's was built of Portland stone in the Regency period of elegant simplicity. In the graceful and light interior is a superb altar-piece of the Last Supper painted by Sir James Thornhill. The artist was born not far away in what is now the White Hart public house, in New Bond Street. His masterpiece remains the great painting inside the dome of St Paul's Cathedral, London.

In total contrast to St Mary's is the Church of St John, beyond the north end of the Esplanade. Since 1859 the tall slender spire of this fine Gothic Revival edifice has reached high over the townscape, a point of reference over a wide area.

The first proper promenade wall was built in 1800, but this had to be completely reconstructed after the catastrophic Great Storm of 1824, which also destroyed much of the villages of Fleet, and Chiswell, Portland. The Esplanade was progressively developed and by 1887 it extended north of Greenhill.

The grid pattern streets of Old Melcombe Regis, at the heart of what is now Weymouth's town centre, dates from medieval times. This view is of St Alban Street.

The weathervane in Greenhill Gardens is a replica of the *Supermarine* aeroplane, a forerunner of the Battle of Britain *Spitfire*. It is a tribute to Weymouth aviator G.H. Stainforth who became the fastest man on earth in the 1931 Schneider speed competition.

For well over 100 years swimmers could change in the many 'bathing machines', which were wheeled into the water all along the beach. Until the Great War undressing in public was frowned upon, and even children on the sands were clothed from head to foot. All such modesty was thrown to the wind after the Roaring Twenties.

The Victorians continued to enhance the Esplanade with traditional seaside features: Beautifully designed cast-iron shelters, the Alexandra and Greenhill public gardens, and the Jubilee Clock, which soon became the popular symbol of Weymouth. It is a central feature on the Esplanade, positioned to catch the eye of tourists arriving from the railway station. Fundraising for the clock tower began in 1887, Queen Victoria's Golden Jubilee year, but most was spent on entertainment and celebrations, leaving only £150 for the clock. A benefactor, Sir Henry Edwards, came to the rescue, and the exuberant unveiling took place the following year. The 15 metre high cast iron tower was made by a Glasgow foundry. In its proper livery (when the town can afford it), it is painted in rich colours, and lavish gilding adorns it ornate mouldings.

The ornately decorated Jubilee Clock has been a focal point on the Esplanade since 1888. It was erected to mark Queen Victoria's Golden Jubilee. Revellers have gathered around this symbolic feature of Weymouth to see in more than one hundred 'New Years'.

Tutankhamen, complete with Egyptian temple and pyramids, appropriately all of sand. Weymouth's sand sculptor Mark Anderson, like his celebrated predecessors, creates his masterpiece tableaux using nothing but natural sand, water and colour.

The Seaside

The second phase of Weymouth's popularity came with the arrival of the railway in 1857. This colourful little train of a different sort takes its passengers along the Esplanade. Behind are the twin pinnacles of the Royal Hotel.

This bronze statue of Queen Victoria - facing her predecessor George III far down the Esplanade - was unveiled by her youngest daughter, Princess Beatrice, in 1902.

concrete legs proved its downfall, and the 3000-tonne pier was demolished in 1986. The original entrance block was left high and dry on the beach, and remains an unsightly interruption to the gentle sweep of the bay. But it does contain a superb restaurant!

Beach entertainment has changed with the times, but simply playing on a warm soft carpet of sand has remained the chief delight through generations of children and adults. The appeal of a Punch and Judy show is universal, and into the twenty-first century. Professor Guy Higgins continues the tradition of this timeless show on Weymouth Sands. Older children like the beach funfair and trampolines, while sports such as beach volleyball have become international events. The town now has a vibrant night-life with numerous pubs, clubs and restaurants, and a multi screen cinema.

As early as 1842 there were hot air balloon trips over the Bay. For exhilaration today visitors can ride inflatable powerboats to the rough white-water off Portland Bill. The water in summer is animated with swimmers, windsurfers and water skiers, and since Victorian times Weymouth Bay and Portland Harbour have been recognised as providing some of the best sailing in the country.

No seaside is complete without its theatres and piers. Weymouth's own theatre – the Pavilion – was built in 1960 on a pier between the Harbour and the seafront. The first theatre on this reclaimed site was a fantastically elegant Edwardian structure made entirely of wood. Perhaps inevitably this burnt down in 1954, in one of the biggest fires the town had seen.

In 1939 a revolutionary new building, projecting over the water at Greenhill, was opened. Throwing tradition to the wind, this short, stubby Art Deco 'Pier Bandstand' was an open-air theatre; sleek, stylish, and lit with 760 metres of neon tubing. Its inadequate

ABOVE Sun, sea and ice-cream – and Punch and Judy on the sands.

LEFT A sail-training ship dressed overall on a 'Tall Ships' visit to Weymouth.

BELOW Weymouth Bay and Portland Harbour offer some of the best sailing in the country.

Along the Wey

UPWEY

The River Wey begins its journey as a series of tiny streams emerging from beneath the hills, the most famous of them at the Wishing Well at Upwey. So narrow is the picturesque Upwey valley, between steep tree-covered hills, that in winter the sun scarcely reaches the lush floor of the ravine.

For more than 500 years the church of St. Laurence has been the valley's focal point. With its tall square bell-tower it is the epitome of the simple but sturdy English country church. George III was among

The River Wey is still a tiny stream where it adjoins Church Street. Yet its mill race is sufficient to power the Upwey Water Mill, seen here, which was built in 1802.

For centuries Upwey Wishing Well has been a magnet for those seeking a little magical power in the clear waters of the natural spring. The Victorians took advantage of this romantic spot by building this two-arched recess into the hillside alongside the spring head. It is now accompanied by beautifully landscaped gardens and a tea room.

countless visitors to make excursions to Upwey and its Wishing Well a centuries-old tradition.

The first of several large water mills on the still small River Wey is just below the Wishing Well. The present building is 200 years old, but a succession of mills on the site can be traced back to the Domesday Book. As well as inspiring Thomas Hardy's story *The Trumpet Major*, the grinding of the mills four pairs of millstones, the ponderous creaking gears of the giant mill wheel, with the endless sound of water tipping

ABOVE The Upwey Valley, here seen from Windsbatch Hill, is one of the most picturesque parts of Dorset.

BELOW St Laurence, Upwey, has the timeless quality of a traditional English country church.

Nottington Spa House is a unique octagonal building erected over a natural sulphurous spring. This was developed in early Victorian times to exploit its water's health-giving properties.

At Broadwey the River Wey divides; one waterway passes through a mill race; the other stream, here, becomes a ford.

from its buckets, adds to the timeless atmosphere of the place.

A little downstream, past the street of cottages at Elwell, the Wey passes some of the most beautiful small mansions in Dorset: These range from Westbrook House (dating from 1620) to the nineteenth century Southbrook, Eastbrook and Upwey houses, each in their own landscaped parkland. These, together with the lofty gabled Upwey Manor (1639) at the junction of Stottingway Street, and numerous smaller buildings are among the hundred or so Listed Buildings in this part of Weymouth.

NOTTINGTON

The Wey flows on through a flood plain to Broadwey, where it becomes a ford – a public highway! Here, part of the stream is diverted under another mill, and meanders on to Nottington.

This village is in two parts, separated by the river. Among the collection of mainly early nineteenth century buildings on the edge of the water meadows is Nottington's mill - the third one on the Wey. Prominent near the junction of the lanes is the great old Malt House, an imposing building of 1834 which retains many of its original features.

On the other side of the river is one of Weymouth's most unusual buildings – the tall octagonal Nottington Spa House. For centuries a spring on this spot was believed to have medicinal – almost magical – healing powers, bringing travellers to sip or wash in its sulphurous waters. Weymouth went into a decline following the death of its patron George III, so in 1830 enterprising folk decided to develop the spa as a paying attraction. For a while it was one of Dorset's most popular attractions, despite the smell of the water being "like the scouring of guns, the taste of a very hard-boiled egg"! By mid-Victorian times spas were no longer fashionable, and it was converted into a private house – whose waters make delicious tea as long as the teapot lid is removed to let the vapour escape!

RADIPOLE

Radipole is one of the few parts of Weymouth mentioned in the Domesday Book. The neighbouring hills give fine views of the lower Wey Valley, now crossed by a bridge carrying the Weymouth Way relief road, but it is difficult to realise that until the 1920s this little flood plain was open to tidal sea water. In its heyday Radipole was probably the site of a Roman port where supplies were landed to be taken via the Roman road to Maiden Castle and Dorchester.

To the north-east of the water meadow lie a trio of historic buildings, all built of Portland Stone; the Old Radipole Manor, the ancient St Ann's Church, and the former village schoolhouse.

The beautiful Elizabethan manor house has mullioned windows and a series of stone gables crowned with carved finials. It is one of the finest and best preserved sixteenth century houses in the area, and its story is embellished with romantic legend. Passed down through the centuries are tales of unholy liaisons between monks and nuns in its long-lost vaults and passages!

Nestling against the Old Manor is the ancient Church of St. Ann, originally the mother-church of Melcombe Regis. It enjoys a cosy setting on the west-facing slope of the Wey Valley, and for some 700 years was a centre of communal activity and worship. Much of the nave dates from about 1250, making it one of the oldest buildings in Weymouth. Subsequent centuries brought extensions to this little church, but mid-Victorian enthusiasm sadly stripped away a few of the original elements. One unusual feature is the Italianate style triple-bell turret. The little tumbling churchyard has many interesting monuments, including some to shipwreck victims.

A few paces across the lane from the church is the old village school, hardly altered since it was built in 1840. Here, lessons behind regimented rows of desks have now given way to the informal glee of pre-school children.

A winding road leads through Radipole village, at its heart a small three-arched bridge over the still narrow River Wey. A sprinkling of simple stone cottages – some thatched, and several secluded larger houses complete the picture. Radipole too has its water mill since the late eighteenth century, hidden from the road near the quiet West End Cottages.

Below Radipole the River Wey used to fan out into a wide water meadow, but it is now channelled into a sharply-cut ditch as part of a 'water management' scheme. Augmented by eight upstream tributaries, the river passes under the Weymouth Way road bridge, and then broadens out into Radipole Lake.

An aquatic place of a different kind lies 2 mile west of the town at Putton Lane. A former industrial area has been transformed into six acres of beautifully landscaped lakes, complete with a replica of a bridge from one of Monet's water lily paintings. Here visitors to Bennetts Water Gardens can admire a world famous collection of water lilies.

Radipole's beautiful Elizabethan Manor House is one of the finest unspoilt sixteenth century houses in Dorset.

The glow of a late evening sun picks out the ancient stonework of the historic Church of St. Ann, Radipole.

Around & About

SUTTON POYNTZ & PRESTON

Picturesque Sutton Poyntz lies at the junction of two streams and is surrounded by hills. More than 1000 years old, it was once a manor with its own church, of which there is now no trace. What do remain are lovely old thatched cottages and willows shading a tranquil duck pond. Nearby are a tall old water mill, and the refreshing presence of the Springhead Inn. Just to the north is a water pumping station which itself is of such interest that it has its own little museum. Displays here tell the story of the Victorians' venture to provide a good piped water so vital to

It is surprising how much rural land remains around such a thriving and built up borough. Here St Andrews Church at Preston can be picked out, still in its village setting. Twentieth century housing development has enveloped much of the south-facing sides of several hills around here.

A beautiful landscape surrounds the tree covered village of Sutton Poyntz. Part of the Ridgeway hill-range, including White Horse Hill, rises on the left.

Weymouth's expanding population. From 1856 water from this wellspring has been pumped to the town and its outlying areas, now at the rate of 12 million litres a day. One remarkable feature is a large cylindrical filter at the well head. This is actually a part of the forward funnel of I.K. Brunel's steamship *Great Eastern* which was damaged by a huge explosion on its trial voyage in 1859. Visitors flocked to see this largest ship in the world while she lay in Portland Harbour under repair.

One of the many pleasant walks from Sutton Poyntz leads to White Horse Hill, where an enormous figure on the chalk hillside depicts George III mounted on his favourite grey charger, which he often preferred to riding in a carriage. The White Horse was cut in 1808, just 3 years after the last of the popular monarch's many visits to the town. Periodical weeding and re-cutting over time has slightly changed the royal profile.

Climbing Plaisters Lane north-westerly from Sutton Poyntz and looking towards Portland, the scene is dominated by Chalbury Hill, crowned by massive earthworks of an Iron Age fort. The climb is steep, but the reward is a breathtaking panoramic

The village pond at Sutton Poyntz. The village is one of Weymouth's most peaceful retreats for residents and visitors alike, and yet it has a vivacious village community.

The White Horse on the hillside between Sutton Poyntz and Osmington was cut in 1808 as a reminder of the visits of King George III who often rode the area on horseback.

A narrow street leads down into the quiet village of Bincombe. The cottages and twelfth-century church rest at the base of an extremely steep hillside below the Ridgeway.

view from Weymouth Bay, over Portland to Lyme Bay and beyond.

The original village of Preston lay in the shallow valley of the Jordon, overlooked by the pretty St Andrew's church. Here and on Jordan Hill to the south have been found the base of a small temple, a cemetery, a hoard of coins, and an intricate mosaic floor of a villa; evidence of an established Romano-British settlement. None of the original settlers would recognize Preston today, for thanks to a series of housing developments the modern village has expanded to cover the surrounding hills.

Old Wyke Regis, still a village at heart.

BINCOMBE

The tiny hamlet of Bincombe is easily overlooked. Served by a single road, and sheltered by the eastern Ridgeway scarp, it is the quietest of all the settlements around Weymouth, lying just outside the borough. Almost untouched for generations, farming is much in evidence on the steep hillsides behind the small cluster of houses and farm buildings. At the eastern end, along an unmade lane, is the secluded church, set in a group of trees. This is a truly ancient building, whose most modern part is the square tower, which was added over 500 years ago.

WYKE REGIS

Until the twentieth century the old village of Wyke Regis, set in a hollow in the landscape, was entirely surrounded by rolling fields. The forming of Portland Harbour accelerated change throughout the area, and had an immense impact on Wyke. In 1891 a huge factory was built on the edge of the Harbour at Ferry Bridge. The Whitehead Torpedo Company pioneered and led the world in the development of torpedoes, and went on to build houses for its workers, a school and community centre. After the Second World War, new housing estates were built over the downland between Wyke, Portland Harbour and the Rodwell side of Weymouth.

Like most ancient settlements Wyke Regis was founded alongside a small watercourse. It was probably well established in Saxon times, growing into a manor with its own Court Leet. In the Middle Ages when the village and its farmlands were a royal demesne (hence the 'Regis' title), the Wyke boundaries encompassed a good part of what is now Weymouth.

Wyke Regis's original church was replaced by the present All Saints' Church in 1455. This is a fine building in the perpendicular style, befitting its original role as the 'mother church' of Weymouth. It is a living church, but upon entering you could be stepping back into the fifteenth century, it has changed so little. The heavy south door is made of thick planks roughly nailed together, and glows with a patina of centuries. Gazing down on the nave are a number of carved figures and faces, including those of Henry VI and his Queen, Margaret of Anjou, who were on the English throne when the church was built. For company they have small effigies of early musicians and craftsmen, pieces recovered from the earlier church on the site.

Wyke Regis church was for centuries an important landmark, especially for mariners navigating past the

All Saints Church, Wyke Regis. Until 1836 this was Weymouth's parish church, and many victims of shipwrecks are buried in the graveyard, including Captain John Wordsworth, brother of the poet William, who was drowned in 1805 when his ship *The Earl of Abergavenny* struck the Shambles.

How many public notices and marriage banns have been pinned to the ancient door of Wyke Regis church? 500 years of continuous use has given a rich patina to the grain of this extremely heavy door.

'Shambles' east of Portland Bill. By aligning the tall square tower with the north east point of Portland, they could avoid that dangerously shallow shoal. What they could not see were the many eerie and fantastic medieval gargoyles guarding higher parts of the building! The gravestones in the large churchyards reflect the lives and events that are etched into the history of this part of Dorset. Notable are exquisitely inscribed monuments to numerous shipwreck and flood victims, and at least one smuggler.

The church stands on rising ground above the old village square, tastefully enlarged by new development in the 1990s. Here the original stream briefly emerges to run through an old horse trough, before disappearing into culverts down to the sea.

Footpaths over the fields to the West of Wyke Regis provide lovely views of the famous Fleet lagoon and Chesil Beach, with the Island of Portland to the south.

Wyke Castle – a rather eccentric name and design for this unique early Victorian dwelling. It looks out over a superb panorama of the Fleet, Chesil Beach and the Island of Portland.

Old Wyke village is now a rich mixture of building styles of many periods. The 400 year-old Manor Farm just west of the church was until the 1980s a rare working survival of the traditional small English farm. The historic features of its enclosed yard, stone sheds and farmhouse have been retained in its conversion to domestic use.

One amazing piece of eccentricity is Wyke Castle. Built some 150 years ago, in an age when classically proportioned architecture was the norm, its designer was clearly a free spirit! Never a castle but a dwelling built for a French doctor, it has a wide circular tower, crenellated walls at odd angles and other unusual features. But it has survived almost unscathed and still enjoys one of the finest views in South Dorset

Remnants of millstones and an ancient fair cross have been found on the hill to the east, reminders of Wyke's rural days, of windmills and village fairs of long ago.

Sandsfoot Castle

The influx of the navy from mid Victorian times brought unprecedented prosperity to Portland and Weymouth during its 150-year presence. Tourism and development boomed, but the building of the Breakwaters also had dramatic and unexpected effects. Currents which had naturally moved waterborne material and accumulated sand along the Weymouth shore of the new harbour, were no more. Weymouth's south-facing coast between Bincleaves and Ferry Bridge had previously been a wide expanse of firm yellow sand, rivalling Weymouth's main beach. Here 'promenaders' would stroll on warm summer evenings, and families could relax in the shelter of the grassy banks. The old road to Portland also went along this shore, to the ferry at Smallmouth Sands where the first bridge to Portland was built in 1839. This waterside road was fed by the main turnpike road from Weymouth, before alternative routes were developed in the early 19th century. Even while the harbour was being formed, most of the sands and the last vestiges of the shore road were already being washed away.

Dominating this southern shore is Sandsfoot Castle, approached through ornamental gardens from Old Castle Road. Before the Breakwaters were built this part of the coast was exposed to the open sea. Consequently south easterly storms eroded the soft stone outcrop on which Sandsfoot Castle had stood since 1539. This historic stronghold was built as part of a chain of coastal defences for Henry VIII. Together with its partner, Portland Castle on the opposite shore, it was designed to cover this vast and important anchorage – a potential landing place for any of Henry's enemies from the Catholic countries.

It was a fine building, with a large octagonal gun platform on its southern side. The walls were so thick that the staircases and privies were contained within them! However, it was abandoned for military use in 1645, and by Georgian times much had disappeared down the receding cliff. There have been many falls since, but enough remains to show the scale and workmanship – some of the worked stone was even recycled from a medieval abbey, although much of the fine ashlar facing has been lost. Odd pieces of tooled masonry can still be found scattered among the rocks below, but the prize exhibit is the carved Royal Coat of Arms from above a gateway, now safe in All Saints' Church at Wyke. The story of Sandsfoot Castle is told in a superb display at its sister, Portland Castle, on the opposite shore of the harbour, which is fully restored and open to the public.

Natural Weymouth

A female bearded tit pecks frantically on the seed head of a reed in Radipole Lake.

RADIPOLE LAKE

Before the 1920s the incoming tide washed up from the Harbour mouth into this wide expanse of shallow water, there meeting the River Wey. In its natural state Radipole Lake was separated from Weymouth Bay by a huge peninsula of sand and shingle. As the old town of Melcombe Regis developed on that spit, a succession of walls and reclamation pushed inward the eastern shores of the lake – and its lower reaches called the Backwater.

Radipole Lake is a wide oasis of natural tranquillity near the heart of the town. It is a superb habitat for many species of birds and other wildlife, and is managed by the Royal Society for the Protection of Birds. On the right is the thatched Information Centre.

ABOVE The ruins of Sandsfoot Castle are still prominent on Weymouth's southern shore, which features several sheltered sandy coves along the Portland Harbour frontage.

BELOW RIGHT The Rodwell Trail is an extremely pleasant green walk between the Town Centre and Ferry Bridge by Portland Harbour. The recently created footpath and cycle track follows the line of the Weymouth to Portland Railway which operated from 1865 to 1965. The curved brickwork of this impressive tunnel is actually a complete ellipse with a hidden inverted arch under the track bed. Notice the platform of the old Rodwell Station.

BELOW Miniature marvels! Exhibitors in the Weymouth International Maritime Modelling Festival show off their finely crafted boats to crowds by the side of Radipole Lake.

The regular drying out of the shallow muddy silt banks in warm weather created a rather unsavoury atmosphere. Victorian attempts to overcome this problem included the construction of a gated weir to maintain the water level in the lake. In 1921 Westham Bridge – actually a dam with sluiced culverts – was built, stopping the sea from entering and turning the former open lagoon into a freshwater lake. For a few years a steam dredger was employed to remove the silt brought down by the River Wey, but by the 1950s large islands of reed beds had formed, the reed being harvested by thatchers.

Fortunately, plans to 'reclaim' the lake for football pitches, car parks and buildings came to nothing, and it is now a major nature reserve. A network of footpaths through its water meadows and dense scrub

Weymouth's bustle is another world to that of Lodmoor – though only recently has its importance been recognized. It is now a nature reserve, and as well as paths, hides have been built so that visitors can observe its flourishing bird and aquatic wildlife.

enable everyone to enjoy this lovely habitat and to study some of the 250 species of bird, some of them rare, which have been recorded here. In spring and summer the air is filled with bird song and calls. Swans, butterflies and dragonflies abound, and even otters may be seen. It is surprising that such a tranquil haven of nature can exist so near the heart of a busy town. The reserve is managed by the RSPB, and expert information is at hand at their centre in the Swannery Car Park.

LODMOOR

Weymouth is fortunate in having two nature reserves. Lodmoor is a true flood plain into which storm waters from the surrounding hills collect. It is almost miraculous that it has survived in its present environment. Horse-racing took place here in the nineteenth century, and from 1849 various attempts were made to drain and reclaim it. The 1920s saw a small aerodrome established, and then half-a-century's worth of the town's rubbish was dumped on it! From the 1930s to the 1970s there were determined efforts to 'develop' it in one way or

another. Plans ranged from a vast 'garden village'; formal sports pitches; a marina with a cut through to the sea, to a vast Butlins holiday camp - which was stopped only after a public inquiry.

Lodmoor, like Radipole Lake, remains a priceless habitat for wildlife, managed by the RSPB. The reserve has beautiful walks, and hides to observe the bearded tits, cettis' warblers, lapwing, and the many waders and other birds which shelter in the surrounding reeds. Lodmoor Country Park also sports an internationally-renowned Sea Life Park. This is a sanctuary for the preservation and study of marine species, including sharks, seals and seahorses, complimented by assorted entertainments and restaurants. Next door the area's attractions are reduced to miniature proportions in the Model World.

Lodmoor is separated from the sea by Preston Beach, a natural ridge of fine shingle through which water could flow – at times in either direction! A nineteenth century wall built in the back of the shingle bank did not prevent the main road behind it from being frequently closed by floods. This was finally resolved when a £6m sea defence scheme was completed in 1996, which included a fine new esplanade which almost doubled the length of Weymouth's sea front promenade.